P9-CQP-300

neighborhoods in nature™

Let's Take a
Field Trip to a
Tide Pool

Kathy Furgang

The Rosen Publishing Group's
PowerKids Press™
New York

For my brother, Steven

Published in 2000 by The Rosen Publishing Group, Inc.
29 East 21st Street, New York, NY 10010

Photo Credits: p. 4 © Animals, Animals; p. 7 © Wayne Green; pp. 8, 9 © Animals, Animals; pp. 10, 11 © Wayne Green; pp. 12, 13 © Animals, Animals; pp. 14, 15 © Wayne Green; pp. 16, 17 © Animals, Animals; pp. 18, 19, 20, 21 © Wayne Green; p. 20 (inset) © Animals, Animals; p. 22 © Wayne Green

Photo Illustrations by Thaddeus Harden

First Edition

Book Design: Felicity Erwin

Furgang, Kathy.
      Let's take a field trip to a tide pool / by Kathy Furgang.
          p.   cm. — (Neighborhoods in nature)
      Includes index.
      Summary: Describes tide pools and the plants and animals that live in them.
      ISBN 0-8239-5446-3 (lib. bdg.)
      1. Tide pool ecology—Juvenile literature. [1. Tide pools. 2. Tide pool ecology. 3. Ecology.] I. Title. II. Series:
Furgang, Kathy. Neighborhoods in nature.
QH541.5.S34F87 1999
577.69'9—dc21
                                                                                                98-55734
                                                                                                     CIP
                                                                                                      AC

Manufactured in the United States of America

Contents

What Is a Tide Pool?

If you walk along the seashore at different times of the day, you will see that the level of the ocean water changes. The water level is highest at **high tide**. The water level sinks down during **low tide**. When tides are low, you can explore the world of tide pools. Tide pools are areas of low, or **shallow**, water surrounded by rock. They are found at rocky seashores, like those in Maine and Oregon. Tide pools act almost like soup bowls in the ground. They collect water left behind from the high tide. They are homes for many beautiful, interesting sea creatures.

◀ *High tide brings waves that crash upon the shore. At low tide, the water goes farther out to sea.*

What Causes the Tides?

Every six hours, ocean tides change. What causes these water levels to move up and down? Tides are caused by the moon. The moon's **gravity** is so strong that it pulls on Earth as Earth turns. Gravity is a natural force that pulls things. The moon's gravity pulls the ocean water out and away from the shore. About six hours later, Earth has turned away from the moon and the pull is not as strong. Without the force of the moon's gravity, the water returns to where it was.

Tides go in and out every night and day. As they do, waves from the tides crash against the ground. Over time, waves make holes in the rocky ground. These holes become tide pools.

High and low tides happen at different times ▶
around the world. Tides change as the sun
and moon rise and set.

What makes starfish special? They have bodies that can fix themselves. When a starfish loses an arm, a new one will naturally grow back in its place. ▶

Who Lives in a Tide Pool ?

8

Most of the sea creatures that live in tide pools are **invertebrates**. Invertebrates have no **backbone**. A backbone is a row of bones that supports an animal's skeleton. Crashing waves that might hurt other animals are not as hard on invertebrates. They are softer and can move easily in water. **Starfish**, **sea anemones**, and **jellyfish** are all invertebrates that live in tide pools. Other invertebrate animals have shells on the outside of their bodies, such as **crabs**, **mussels**, and **clams**. Simple plants, such as **moss** and **seaweed**, also live in ocean tide pools.

A Hard Place

to Survive

Tide pools are not easy neighborhoods for animals to live in. Imagine being a tiny sea creature. Twice a day, waves hit you and cover you for hours. Then the water goes away. Only a small pool is left and you almost dry up in the hot sun. That's what it is like for tide pool animals.

Animals such as crabs and starfish, can be found in other areas of the ocean, but for those that live in a tide pool, it is often the only life they know. They were born in a tide pool and spend their whole lives in a tide pool.

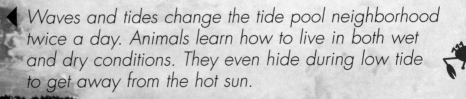

Waves and tides change the tide pool neighborhood twice a day. Animals learn how to live in both wet and dry conditions. They even hide during low tide to get away from the hot sun.

How Animals in Tide Pools Eat

Each animal in a tide pool eats in a different way. Crabs have claws that they use to grab food. Sea anemones have feelers that sting and poison fish, so that the fish stop moving. When the fish are still, the anemones can suck them into their mouths. Starfish, mussels, and clams eat seaweed and other tiny sea creatures made up of only one cell.

Acadian Hermit Crab

Horned Starfish

When high tide comes, it's mealtime! Animals must find as much food as possible before the tide goes out again.

12

Blue Mussels

True Tulip Snail

These creatures are so small that humans walking along the beach cannot see them. The animals in a tide pool don't run out of food to eat because the ocean waters carry food from tide pool to tide pool.

Beadlet Anemone

Green Sea Anemone

13

The Splash Zone

The seashore is divided into different tide pool areas that are called zones. The zone farthest from the deep ocean is called the **splash zone**. This area is dry and rocky and does not get covered in water. Tide water only reaches it with splashes and mist. Very few sea animals can live here because there is not enough water. Animals, such as crabs, wander into the splash zone for food but they have to be fast. They are easy to see without the water to cover them, and seagulls or other larger animals can eat them.

Seals like the splash zone because they can relax on ▶
rocks and go into the water to find their food.

Purple Sea Urchin

Triton Trumpet Snail approaches Sea Urchin

North Atlantic Green Sea Urchin

16

The Low Zone

The area of the tide pool that gets the most water is the low zone. The **low zone** is closest to the deep ocean, so when the tide comes in, it covers the low zone with water first. When the tide goes out, this area is the last to be left uncovered. A few animals that live here are sea slugs, sea spiders, and small **sea urchins**. Waves are hard on most small animals, but the sea urchin has a special trick to stay alive. It carves a hole in the rocks with its hard shell. The urchin then goes inside the rock to stay safe from the crashing waves.

These colorful urchins have mouths with tiny rows of teeth inside. ▶

17

The Mid-Tide Zone

The **mid-tide zone** is found in the middle of the tide pool area. This is the most active zone of all because many animals live here. Even more animals come here looking for food, as the tides move in and out. Starfish, sea anemones, and mussels are just a few of the animals that live in the mid-tide zone. Like most shelled sea animals, mussels eat by sucking ocean water in and out of their bodies. When the water leaves their bodies, tiny one-celled animals from the water stay behind. These one-celled animals are food for the mussels. All tide pool animals use the ocean to meet their needs.

◀ *Have you ever seen empty shells at the seashore? They are empty because the animal that once lived in it died or left it to find a bigger shell as a new home.*

19

The High Zone

Tide pools are one of the most interesting places to watch sea life. You can get up close and watch communities of fish, plants, and animals.

The **high zone** is farthest from the deep ocean. It has the biggest changes from high tide to low tide. Only the toughest creatures can survive here. When the tide comes in, animals in the high zone can find the food they need. When the tide is out, they have trouble staying alive. There is no food, little water, and the sun is very hot.

Crabs and snails live here. They eat seaweed and tiny creatures. Their shells protect them from being eaten. Their shells also protect them from burning in the hot sun during low tide.

21

Exploration
Field Trip to a
Tide Pool

If you have ever explored a tide pool, you were probably looking in the splash zone or the high zone. You can see wonderful animals in these areas. You may see crabs walking along the rocks with their shells on their backs. Do not get too close to the animals, however. It can be dangerous to touch sea creatures that are alive. Jellyfish sting, and crabs pinch and bite. Sea creatures depend on their salty ocean neighborhood to stay alive, so don't touch or move them. Just stand by quietly and watch the incredible world of tide pools.

Web Sites

You can learn more about tides and tide pools at these Web sites:

http://octopus.gma.org/katahdin/tidepool.html

http://www.umassd.edu/public/people/kamaral/thesis/tidepools.html

Glossary

backbone (BAK-bohn) A spine, or a row of bones, in an animal's back that supports its skeleton.

clam (KLAM) An invertebrate with a soft body inside two shells.

crab (KRAB) An invertebrate with eight legs, two claws, and a shell.

gravity (GRAH-vih-tee) The force that comes from a massive object that pulls things towards it, such as the moon's pull on Earth's oceans.

high tide (HY TYD) The time when ocean water is highest on the shore.

high zone (HY ZOHN) The part of a tide pool area that has the biggest changes between low and high tide.

invertebrate (in-VUR-tih-brit) An animal without a backbone.

jellyfish (JEH-lee FISH) A soft, invertebrate animal that can sometimes sting.

low tide (LOH TYD) The time of day when ocean water is lowest on the shore.

low zone (LOH ZOHN) The area of a tide pool that gets the most water.

mid-tide zone (MID-TYD ZOHN) The tide pool area where a lot of animals find food.

moss (MOSS) Tiny green plants that grow in clumps.

mussel (MUH-sul) An invertebrate with a soft body inside two shells.

sea anemone (SEE uh-NEH-muh-nee) A soft, brightly-colored sea animal that looks like a flower.

sea urchin (SEE UR-chin) A small sea animal with a hard shell and spines.

seaweed (SEE-weed) A group of many kinds of green plants that grow in the ocean.

shallow (SHA-loh) Not deep.

splash zone (SPLASH ZOHN) The tide pool area closest to the land. It gets water from the splashes of ocean waves.

starfish (STAR FISH) An invertebrate sea animal that is shaped like a star.

23

Index

Patterson Elementary
3731 Lawrence Dr.
Naperville, IL. 60564